faces
IN PLACES

faces
IN PLACES

Compiled by Jody Smith

First published 2010 by
Ammonite Press
an imprint of AE Publications Ltd,
166 High Street, Lewes, East Sussex, BN7 1XU

Reprinted 2011

ISBN 978-1-906672-90-4

Compiler: Jody Smith
Editor: Richard Wiles
Designer: Adam Carter

Colour reproduction by GMC Reprographics

Printed and bound in China by 1010 Printing International Ltd

CONTENTS

INTRODUCTION

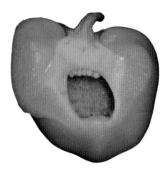

Faces are brilliant! Without them we couldn't smile, laugh, frown, scowl or scream. But they're not always attached to a head. In fact, this book will make you believe they're more commonly attached to bath tubs, shoes and biscuits, among other things.

That's because faces are everywhere. And if you don't believe me, look around. There's probably a face staring at you right now...

Faces in Places started life on my camera: a few random objects I'd idly snapped when out and about that resembled faces. I posted them on the photo sharing website Flickr and suddenly realised I wasn't alone in spotting faces on inanimate objects. I invited other face-spotters to contribute their photos to an online group until it grew to be so big that I decided there had to be a way to showcase the very best finds.

So I launched the **Faces in Places** blog in 2007 and suddenly a movement was born. Photos flooded in faster than I could blog them and now more than 4,000 people have contributed around 20,000 photos to the website.

This book features the finest, funniest and most intriguing faces, and I'm hoping it will make you grin from ear to ear – not only because it's 100% awesome, but also because 10% of profits go to charity. Hope For Children helps disabled, orphaned, poor and exploited children by assisting their rights to basic necessities, such as education and health care. So thanks for putting a smile on a child's face by buying it!

For more faces in places (and to submit your own) visit:
www.facesinplaces.biz

Enjoy the book and happy face hunting!

Jody Smith

Chapter 1

Express Yourself

This rogue's gallery of emotionally charged faces displays a range of expressions from curiosity, amusement and frivolity, to surprise, boredom, unabashed love and happiness.

Plane happy

Puckering petals

Check out my decking dentistry!

I'm a shaaaark!

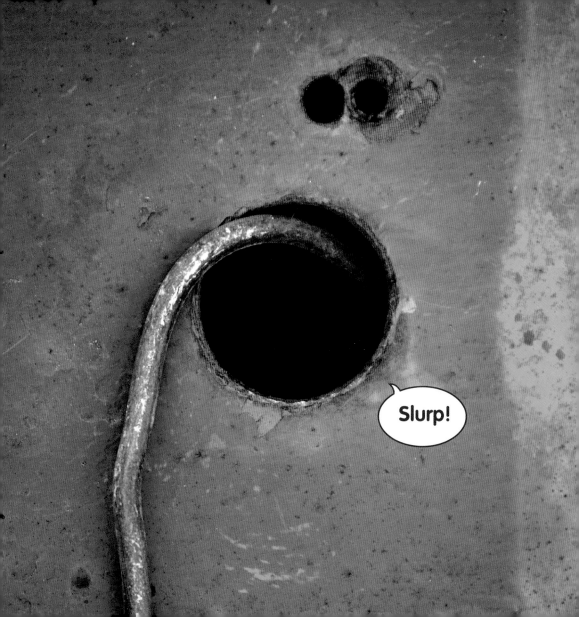

Tree sad

Tiki time

Cable guy

Mop 'n' roll stars

Post daze

Road rage

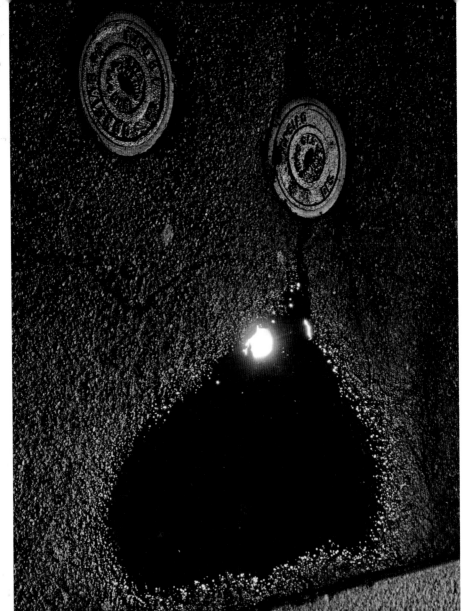

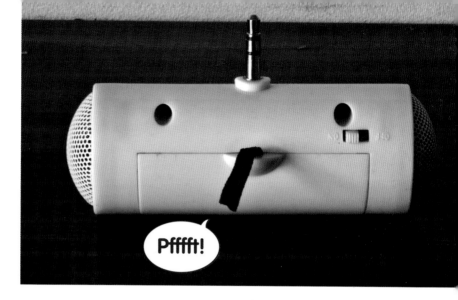

Picky
tastes

Ahoy there, land lubber!

We come from a land down under

Mr Blobby

Control freak

Red-eye reduction

Head in the clouds »

Chapter 2

Happy And Sad

Giggling, smirking or exuberantly happy faces are to be found everywhere – but amid the guffaws and belly laughs, there are also some characters who could really do with a hug.

Bag of laughs

Iron man

High flyer

That sinking feeling

Queasy rider

Tub girl

Good times

Bad times

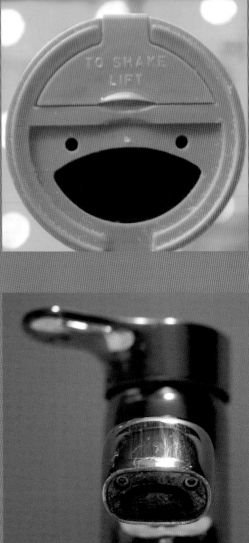

Ol' Sad Eyes

Happy man bag

Toothy grin

Smiley bubbles

Sooo board

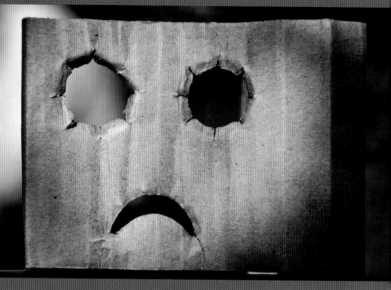

Feeling grate

Wired for sound

Don't worry, tree happy

Yikes!

Self-satisfied smirk

**Worry
bot**

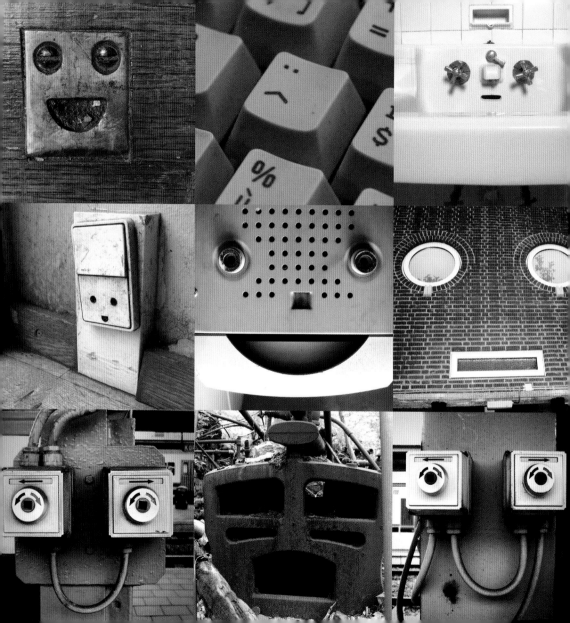

« **The great depression**

Hooked on you

Chapter 3

Name That Face!

Can you name the everyday objects that the following faces belong to? Test your friends; and if you're stuck, turn the page upside down for the answer. No cheating! You're being watched.

① ☆ Sit on my face

② Get a grip

1 Chair cushion 2 Running machine handle

˄ Furry friend ③

A real sucker ④

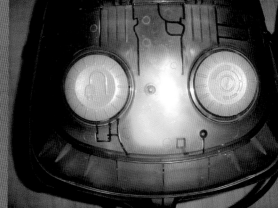

Keeps it together

1 Stapler

Bright eyes no more

❶ The doorman

❷ Plinky plonky

❸ Open-and-shut case

❹ Well connected

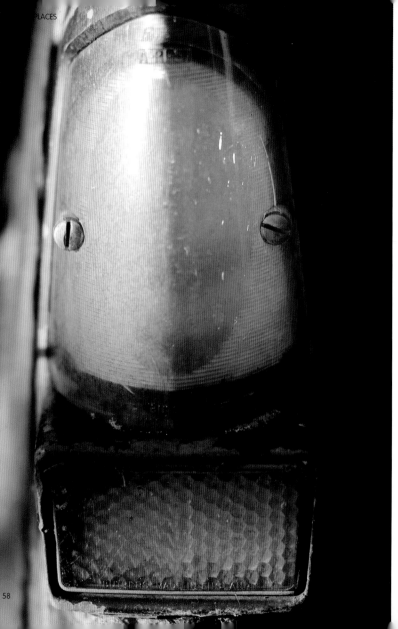

① **Which way now?**

② » **What's the link?**

1 Car indicator 2 Bike chain

1 **It burns!**

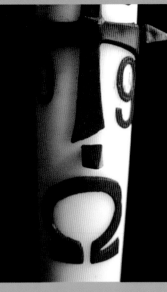

2 » **Don't get caught**

3 **I need a drink**

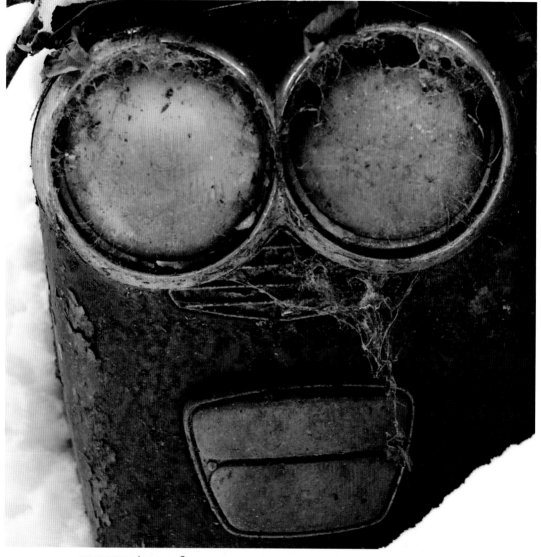

① **Fancy a tune?**

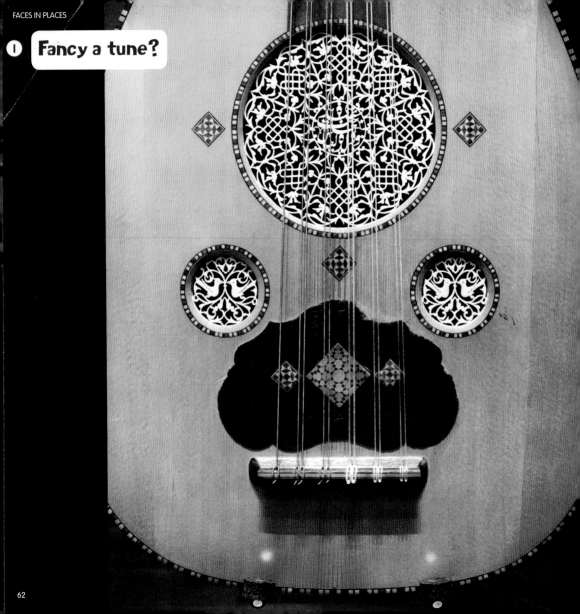

② ⌣ **Wee don't know him**

③ **Motor mouths**
④

① **Airy eyeballs**

1 Car ventilators 2 Saucepan handle

② **Can you handle it?**

1 **Junk food diet**

② **Fancy a brew?**

❶ He's been framed!

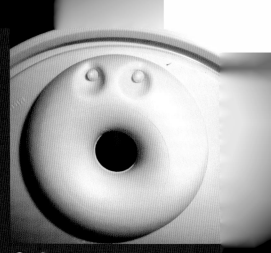

❷ Gone potty

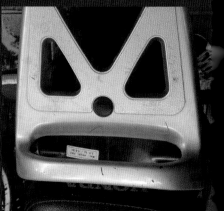

❸ No staple diet

❹ Quick rack

⑤ **Nosey round the back**

Chapter 4

Street Mates

Never feel alone when out for a walk – there are friendly faces watching you everywhere, on buildings, road signs, fire hydrants, advertising hoardings and other street furniture.

Battlement buddy

Whistlin' dixie

Brace yourself!

A troubled sign

Whadda I do?!

Mellow yellow

« **Mr Nosey on the look out**

Green giant

In fine song

Sly house watches your every move

Beware...

...of the samurai

Terrace triplets

Car gobbler

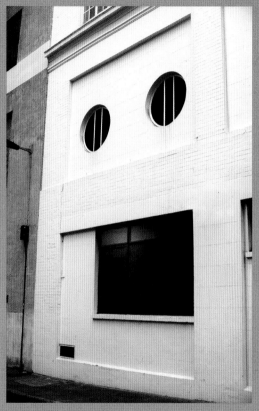

Shouting shop

TELEPHONE

recycle here…

Bin there, done that

Skully

Superior streetlamp is unimpressed

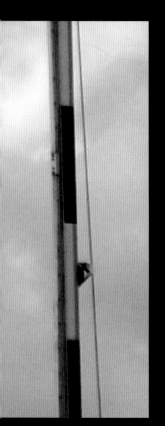

**Sneakybot
waits for the
right moment**

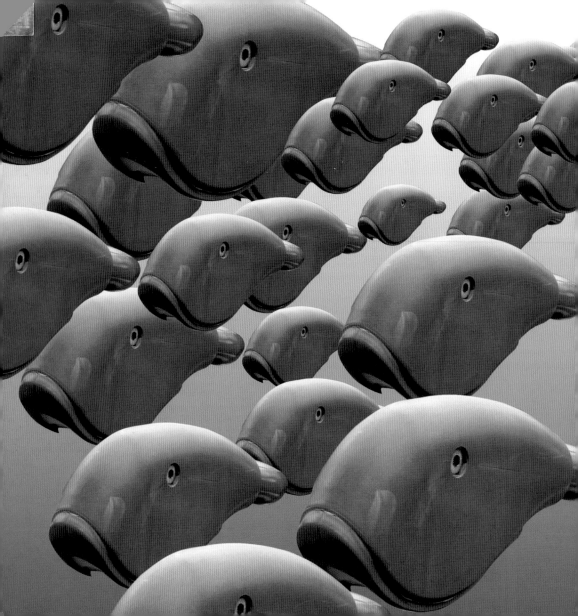

Chapter 5

Creature Features

Welcome to the secret zoo, a menagerie of objects with faces that resemble our friends in the animal kingdom, whether it's a snapping reptile, a curious rodent, a fish or a fowl.

Walkies!

Shark attack!

Shoal of trolleys

His bark's worse than his bite

I am the walrus

Don't startle the lizard...

...yikes!

Angling for the angry fish

Cookie monster

Robo crab

Elephant man

A purrrfect family...

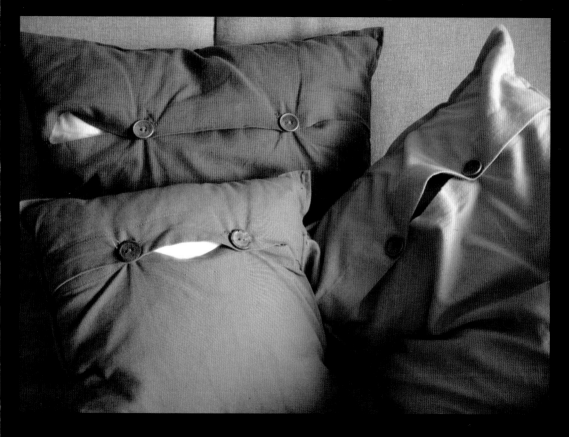

Birds on a wire

« **Dino-saw-us**

CREATURE FEATURES

« **Happy as a pig in mud**

Sloth love chunk!

Zipper fish

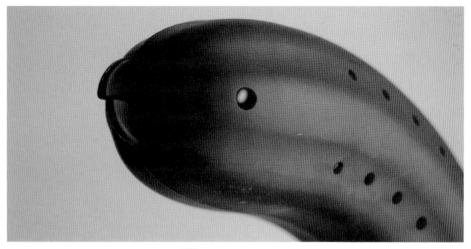

˅ Bunny block

˄ Tweety bird

˅ Ribbit!

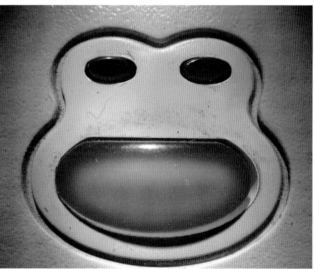

The crow

Guppy's barking mad

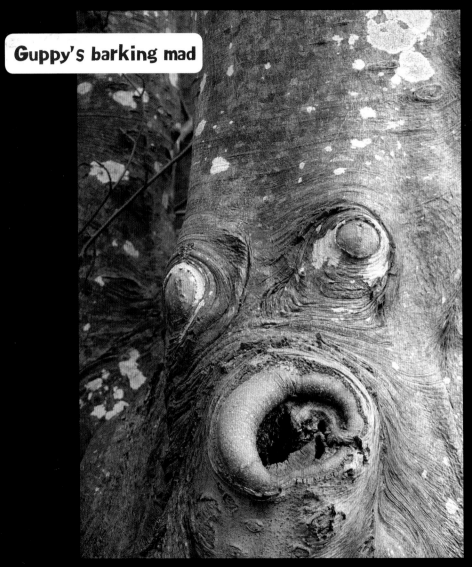

Beaver takes a nap

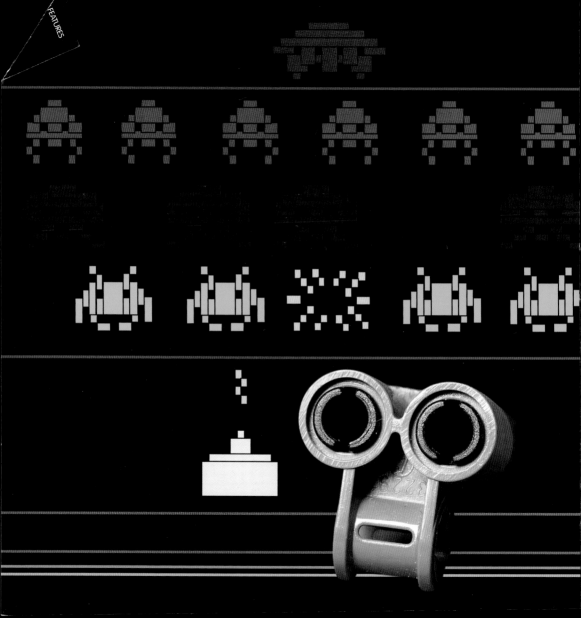

Chapter 6

Face Invaders

The invasion has already begun! Alien beings are infiltrating our everyday life, and if you're vigilant you'll be able to spot their faces in appliances, machines or concealed in nature.

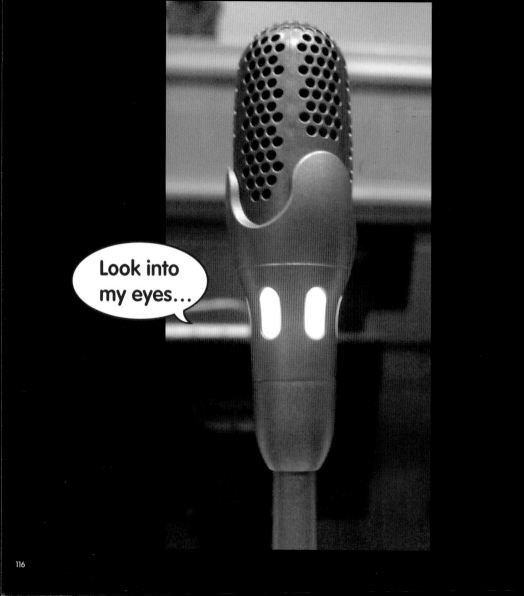

Medusa!

Gobby bot

˅ Ghostly sucker

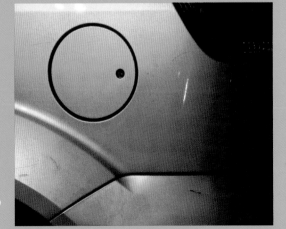

˅ Merging into the foliage

Fuelled up

Mad as hell

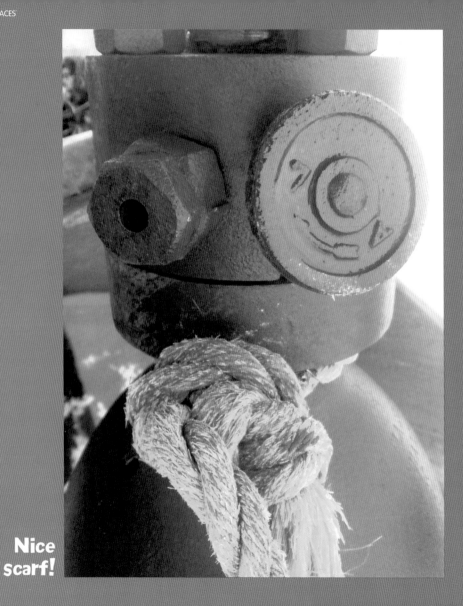

**Nice
scarf!**

Stony stares

Lady Liberty

Plug me in

Bowie-eyed bot

Stealth bin disapproves of your litter

The cash man

Pan man

Plane features

Look out (for faces) wherever you are!

Chapter 7

Shock and Awe!

Surprise! Surprise! These characters really didn't see you coming, if their startled reactions – registering panic and amazement, disbelief and confusion – are anything to go by.

Pink panic

Hell's bells!

You did what?

Nooo!

Who you calling big nose?

Shock rock

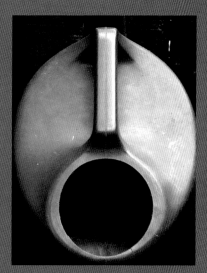

The Scream

Scary movie

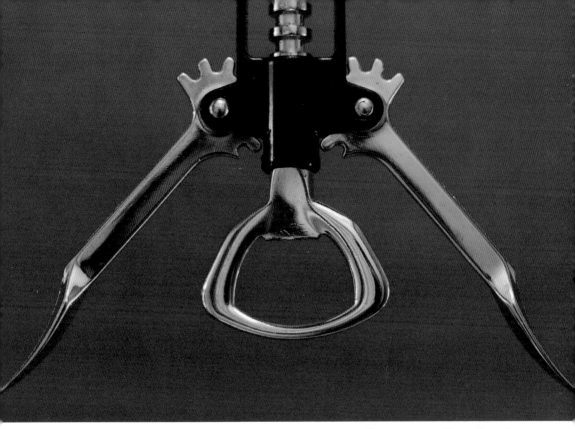

Screwed in the head

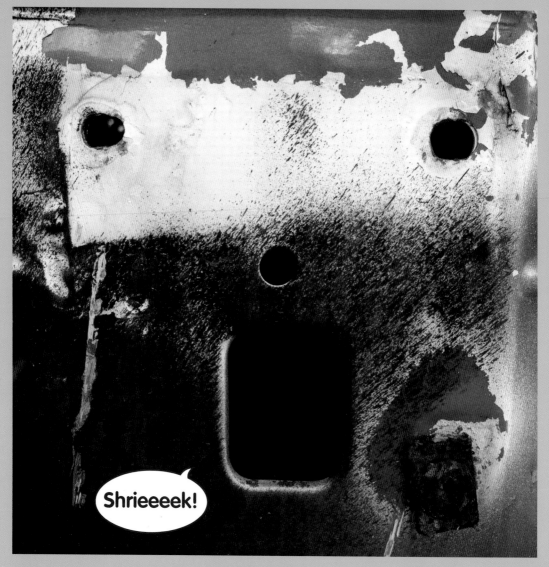

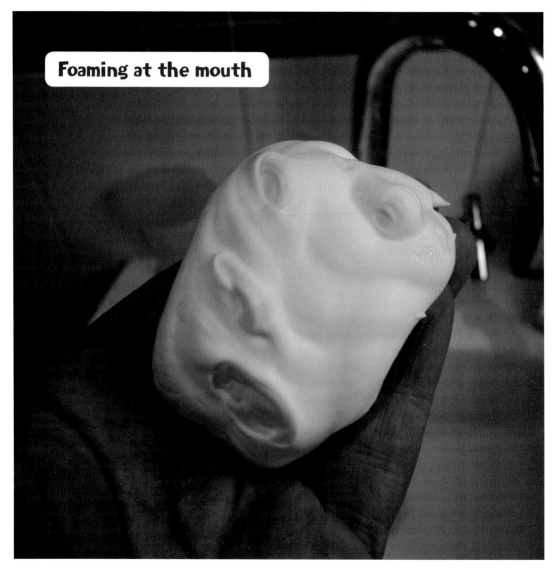

Foaming at the mouth

Getting the measure

You woodn't?

Confusion has a face

Chapter 8

You Are What You Eat

Think twice before sinking your teeth into your dinner. Chances are, your food may bite back! Here's a feast of faces found in fruit and veg, cakes and cookies, and other delightful dishes.

Tomat-oh!

Dr Pepper wants your brains for breakfast

**The
ice man
cometh**

**Do you
know the
muffin
man?**

Pool paaaarty!

The curious orange

Spud brothers

He's the icing on the cake

⌄ Crooked cookies

⌃ Sleepy dumpling

Cabbage patch kid

Pretzel approves of your wine selection

Chatty chestnut

Smoothie operator

Sweet lips

Crabby apple

Farfalle fear

Avocadose

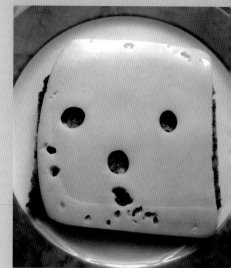

The Baby Cheeses

Nutty stare